Raise Your Vibration For Ascension

– A Guide to Help You Vibrate High

By Laura Anne Whitworth

Copyright© 2019 by Laura Anne Whitworth

About the Author

Laura Anne Whitworth is a Quantum Healing Hypnosis Practitioner (QHHT®) trained in the hypnosis methods of the late, great Dolores Cannon. Laura is based in Chesterfield which is in Derbyshire in the United Kingdom. As well as practicing Quantum Healing for clients up and down the UK, Laura is also a fulltime Mother to two children.

This work included, Laura is the author of 'Isadora Stone and the Magic Portal' available on Amazon. This is a fiction book based on disclosure topics and the imminent Ascension of planet Earth, aimed at young adults. Laura is also the author of 'Prepare Yourself For Hypnosis – A Guide to Visualisation Mastery' also available on Amazon.

Laura has a YouTube channel where she discusses incredible information regarding the Ascension of Planet Earth that has been derived from Quantum Healing sessions. She also shares her latest opinions on the energies coming into the planet and disclosure topics.

You can find Laura online on her Laura Whitworth YouTube channel or alternatively on her Facebook page which is 'Quantum Healing Hypnosis Chesterfield with Laura Whitworth'.

Alternatively if you would like to book a Quantum Healing Hypnosis Session with Laura please email lauraanne.webb@gmail.com

Ascension

Our Planet is ascending to the Fifth Dimension.

What does this mean?

It means that Earth or Gaia as she is called, is ready for her next evolutionary jump in consciousness. A Quantum Leap. And her consciousness is moving to the Fifth Dimension. Our Earth is a living sentient being. And we are all one. All part of the one. The great creator. All of the beings that currently live on Earth are being invited to make this great move with her. And at a soul level everyone has already decided whether they will be making the move to the Fifth Dimension or not. If you are reading this book then I am guessing that you have booked a ticket for team Ascension! The greatest show in the Universe. The Fifth Dimensional move that Gaia will be making is positively polarised. This means that in order to make the Ascension leap with her, we need to be positively polarised too.

What does that mean? How does one become positively polarised?

There are lots of elements to this. But one of the most fundamental, essential parts to being positively polarised is being of 'service to others'. Now by this, I don't mean always be running around after other people and putting yourself last. That is not what I mean at all. You cannot pour from an empty cup. You must always look after yourself and keep your physical and emotional wellbeing at the core of all you do. However, being 'service to others' in my world simply means 'kindness'.

In my daily life, every day, in every situation, I always look for the opportunity to be kind. To show kindness. In the world that we live in, along the way, kindness seems to be forgotten about all too often.

I walk down a street and I smile and say hello to everyone I encounter. Some will ignore me for fear that they have been noticed by someone. 'What's the catch?' they think as crimson colour flashes up their cheeks and they draw their hood around their faces a little tighter. But some will smile back and say hello. Their entire countenance changes. They have been shown kindness and it has given them the opportunity to show kindness back. Then the next person they themselves encounter will receive the benefit of their good mood. All because of a smile and a kind word. We are lighting people up with our light and they in turn are passing the flame.

I frequent supermarkets a lot with my children and I always intuitively pick a queue where I think a smile and a kind word is needed. I talk to people. I look people in the eyes when they speak and I really listen to them. Why do I do this? I do it because I care. I care about people. I see the weight of the world on most people's shoulders. They are so worn down by life in this 3D realm with all its trials and tribulations that they have forgotten how to smile. How to feel joy. How to be in joy. Most people in this world are unaware that they signed a soul contract to be here before they incarnated. Most people are unaware that we are eternal beings that live on and on. We have all of us lived hundreds or thousands of times as individualized pieces of consciousness, split off from the Creator. Inside of us we all have a spark of light that is a piece of the Source. Source or God or Creator, however you choose to identify with the one true light, is all that there is. As individualized pieces of the Source, we incarnate in these human suits that we wear for the experience.

For the soul growth. For the expansion. We live over and over again. We do this to 'know ourselves'. As one of my clients once said in a Quantum Healing Session, 'We have to be blind when we incarnate on Earth, so we can learn how to see.'

We keep coming back to learn our lessons. To pay back Karma that we owe. As we accumulate the soul growth from our lessons learnt in the physical realm, our consciousness expands and our vibration rises. Earth is known in the Cosmos as one of the hardest places to incarnate.

The Ultimate goal is to ascend back to Source through a journey of consciousness and take all of the lessons that we have learnt on our journey back to Source. To the All that Is. So that Creator can 'know itself.' So that Creator can understand Love.

Would people in our world be a little kinder to each other if they knew that we are here in lesson? Would they be kinder to each other if they all recognized that we are all one? That each of us are helping the other learn the lessons that we need to learn in order for our souls to grow?

Each of us on the Earth right now are on our own journey. We are taking our little spark on a journey through consciousness. And through the lessons we encounter and learn from, we will eventually ascend back through the dimensions to Source.

An opportunity is coming.

For those of us who are ready for the next evolutionary step, to make the jump to the next dimension of consciousness. The 3rd dimension is heavy and focused on Duality. Black and White. There is pain and suffering. There is also Love. The 5th Dimension I am told in my Quantum Healing Sessions is like 'Heaven on Earth.' This dimension is beautiful. It is full of love. Everyone respects each other. All of the lower dimensional traits that we are allowed to practice in Duality such as Jealousy, Anger, Spite, Envy. Hate etc. do not exist in this dimension. In this dimension we work together. There is telepathy and we are connected to each other through thought. There is telekinesis and people can move things with their minds.

There is also I am told (and have experienced myself in a QHHT® Session) the ability to fly. Some people when I have hypnotized them have experienced being able to swim under water. There are Mermaids and Fairies and Dragons in the 5th Dimension. There is an overwhelming feeling of Love and acceptance for all. When I listen to my clients describing this place with such awe and reverence in my sessions, I so long myself to experience this.

Before I trained in QHHT®, I myself had a session. I experienced two 'normal' Earth lives and my final life I saw myself on New Earth after the Ascension to 5D had happened. I was living in the trees with my family. My husband had asked a circle of trees if we could live within them and they had gladly agreed and formed themselves into the shape of a bowl, and when we wanted somewhere to have some 'down time' this is where we went. I saw my children flying with fairies and visiting the mermaids. I saw myself blissfully happy and looking incredible! It seems in the Fifth Dimension you can express yourself in any way you like in the physical form and my body looked pretty good! We spent all day going on adventures and exploring. The trees where we lived were full of crystals which helped us communicate with other beings and if we wanted to we could connect telepathically to others who also lived there. It was quite simply put – paradise.

So how do we get to this place of paradise? How does this happen? How does it work?

We are moving into the Age of Aquarius. We are leaving the dark ages and moving into the Light. Our Galaxy is moving into a place within the Universe that contains more light, and so this light in turn effects our frequency.

Energies of high frequency light emanating from our Galactic Central Sun have been washing over the planet now for some time. Slowly raising our frequencies. I am told in my sessions that it has to happen this way, little by little so our circuits are not fried. Every new light wave that comes in is raising your vibration more and also upgrading your DNA. Our DNA is upgrading so we have the necessary 'equipment' to 'come online' when we move to the Fifth Dimension. When these waves of energy come in and wash over the planet the energy wave's effect different people in different ways. Some people (myself included) feel very tired and have no energy at all when the waves come in. It makes others who are more negatively polarized or contain a greater level of negativity in them, feel angry or anxious. What these waves are encouraging us to do, is address our negativity or traumas, face them, heal them, send them love and then release them. Those of us that are 'working on ourselves' are constantly looking at our past traumas and healing them in order to release that trapped negative energy so we can rise with the vibration of the planet. This is where past life regression comes in as a lot of people have trapped traumas still within their coding in their DNA that aren't even from this current lifetime. We all have a lot of healing to do. **And as we heal, we rise**. But sometimes first you need to know what it is you have to heal before you can heal it, which is why I love doing the job I do as I am helping people do this.

For the people who aren't aware of this and are not working on healing their previous traumas. As they are retaining this negativity within them and not healing it, they are moving further and further away in polarization from the people who are working on healing. As the light waves come in and the people working on themselves rise higher and higher. The people who aren't working on themselves are being pulled further and further in the opposite direction. This is ultimately when 'the big wave' that comes is going to cause a splitting of the collective consciousness into two different dimensions. There are those who are ready for the evolutionary jump to the 5th Dimension and those who are not and need more time in the 3rd Dimension in order to learn their lessons. When I say 'learn their lessons' there is no judgement there at all. We are all in lesson. But some of us are ready to graduate to the next level and some of us still need more time in order to understand and process everything. Much like at school you have people who will progress through certain subjects quicker than others. Other people need more time on that level of that particular subject in order to fully understand that level. Remember this is all about soul growth. Our soul in eternal. It has eternity to work through these levels and understand everything. So some are ready now, and some need more time to experience more duality within the 3rd Dimension.

So what is this 'big wave' I talk about? Some describe it as a 'wave of light' that emanates from the Galactic Central Sun within our galaxy. For me, I'm inclined to believe that this wave is triggered from within side ourselves when our consciousness reaches a certain level of vibration. But whatever you choose to believe this 'wave' is, the one thing that everyone says in my sessions is that when it arrives it changes everything. It tips those who are already vibrating high into resonating with the 5th Dimension and from this point on this is what you will see.

I am told that this wave will come as a shock to some, as they did not know it was coming. Some are choosing to undertake the shift in consciousness whilst still 'asleep.' Meaning that they are not aware that Ascension is even a 'thing!' They are good people who are positively polarized and practice service to others. They are of a vibration that is high enough to resonate with the new dimension and therefore they go there. But when this big change happens for these people, it will come as a shock, as they didn't know it was coming. I am told these are the people that will need our support. In one of my sessions a client described these people as 'the sleepers who arrived here who are very dazed and confused, but have big smiles on their faces.' I'll bet!

So whether the wave is Light that emanates from the grand central sun, or whether it comes through the portal inside our hearts inside of us. However this wave will arrive. It is coming. More and more people are gaining an awareness of this. More and more people are coming for QHHT® sessions to identify and heal trapped pain so their vibration rises. More and more people are training as QHHT® Practitioners. All in preparation for the big wave and the Ascension of planet Earth. The wave that will tip our already high frequency up into resonating with the Fifth Dimension.

No-one knows for sure when this big wave will arrive.

But whenever it arrives, we need to be ready.

We need to be Vibrating High.

We need to be in Joy.

We need to be sharing Love.

In my Quantum Healing Sessions so many clients give details on this energy wave. And every time when they do I ask the same question.

What can we do to prepare for when the big energy wave comes?

And here is what I am told...

Diet

I cannot stress enough the importance that diet plays in raising your vibration and keeping it high. This is normally the first thing that is mentioned by a clients 'Higher self' during hypnosis sessions when I ask what they need to be doing in order to get themselves ready for ascension. It seems that our diet is one of the biggest things that can affect our vibration. What we are constantly putting into our bodies on a daily basis has a direct effect on the vibration of our body.

In the world that we live in our pineal glands have become calcified through the water that we drink which contains fluoride and the metals that are ingested by us daily.

We all need to have de-calcified pineal glands in order to be able to access our inner vision. However regardless of this as a goal, we should not be drinking water that is full of fluoride anyway as it is not good for our bodies.

The following are the changes to diet that I hear from clients when they are under hypnosis and we are speaking to their 'higher selves.' They are the changes suggested to raise ones vibration. They are also good lifestyle changes to make in general to ensure health and vitality.

- Drink good quality water daily that is fluoride free. You can achieve this through a water distiller or a good quality water filter. Mineral water is also a good quality water providing it does not contain fluoride. If you are going to use a water distiller please also research what minerals you need to add in order to ensure that you are not lacking in minerals as the Distiller will take everything out including the good stuff! Drink plenty of water daily.

- Include a slice of lemon or fresh herbs in your water if you don't like the taste of pure water. Bless your water before you drink it and infuse it with white light from Source. I do this by placing my hands over the water and visualising white light coming out of my palms and into the water.
- Eat food that contains 'Light'. By this I mean food that is grown from the Earth itself and not food that is light in terms of weight. The 'Light' that the food contains gives you additional life force and energy. Things that grow using the love from our Sun and the water from our Earth contain LIFE. The more of this life force that you ingest, the better you will feel. Anything that is grown with Light and Water will raise your vibration. I also bless my food and give thanks for it whilst cooking it and before eating it. I feel genuine gratitude for the life of the vegetables that I am preparing and I thank them for the role they will play in keeping me alive. Too much of our society nowadays takes things for granted. We go to supermarkets and everything is laid out for us in neat little plastic packages and we think that's where food begins its journey. It doesn't. It has a life. It has consciousness. We must feel true gratitude for our food.
- Cook with Coconut Oil (Caprylic Acid). Caprylic Acid is excellent for ridding your body of candida and fungus. I would also suggest physically ingesting a spoonful of Coconut Oil daily (if you can stomach it!) and prior to swallowing it, pulling it through your teeth as it is very good for killing bacteria in the gums too.

- Cook with colourful vegetables and fruits flavoured with natural spices and herbs. Having a robust spice and herb cupboard is of paramount importance to your health. I would also suggest having a little herb garden with fresh herbs growing. Everyone can do this you do not need a garden. You can even buy the herbs already grown form the supermarket. It's a small change that will make a massive difference to your overall health.
- Take a spoonful of Apple Cider Vinegar Daily. Apple Cider Vinegar is excellent for ridding your body of Candida and Fungus and it is also great for de-calcifying your Pineal Gland.
- We really need to get a handle on what we are putting into our bodies. A great way to do this is to grow your own organic produce. If this is not an option for you, try and buy organic produce from the supermarket if you can afford it. Remember to raise your vibration you need to think about the vibration of the food you are ingesting yourself. Has it had a happy life? If not you are ingesting that negative vibration into your body. Is it covered in Pesticides? Pesticides will not raise your vibration.
- A great way for you to control what you are putting in your body is to cook your own food. Microwave meals are full of sugar and salt and chemicals which are not good for our bodies or our vibration. If you are preparing your own food you can regulate what is going in it.
- Take Probiotics to put back good bacteria in your gut. Unfortunately with the antibiotics that we have all taken over the years and with the increase in Candida overgrowths, our good bacteria in our guts have taken a hit. You can buy live probiotics in yoghurt drinks, or you can buy Probiotics in tablet form.

- Add Epsom salts to your daily bath. Epsom salts are very good for the body to help it detoxify. It can also replenish your Magnesium stores which can be drained through a stressful lifestyle in today's world. It also promotes more restful sleep. Ensure you do a patch test on your skin to check you are not allergic before you thrown a tonne in the bath!
- Diatomaceous Earth (Food Grade) is an excellent way of moving metals out of your body that are stored in the various tissues. I take this in tablet form and found that this really worked for me. After taking two weeks' worth of Diatomaceous Earth I felt like a new woman. You shouldn't take this continuously though and must give your body a rest period every now and then. Make sure you read the packaging for instructions on how to take Diatomaceous Earth.
- If you can afford it, try and eat Organic Produce. You are directly ingesting the vibration of the food that you eat. You want to be eating food that has had a good life and is happy!
- Also I am told time and time again that we need to be reducing the amount of meat in our diets, ideally to just eating a portion of Chicken and Fish once a week if we do in fact eat meat at all. I know this is a contentious topic as lots of people enjoy eating meat. Everybody is different. And every one has different needs and requirements in order to keep their bodies functioning in the physical. Up to being in my 30's I was a voracious meat eater. My husband and I travelled all the length of Route 66 on our honeymoon and we had a burger or a steak in every city! Since beginning my work as a Quantum Healing Practitioner I no longer eat meat and now choose to eat a Vegetarian diet. I chose to do this for me as I often get clients who will go into past lives where they lived as animals.

This has totally changed my outlook on the consumption of animals. I ate meat daily for years and now I cannot bear the thought of it. I am told however by the 'higher selves' that I speak to that if we must eat meat and ingest this into our bodies. Choose to eat an animal that has had a good life. As this will affect the animal's vibration. Remember everything is vibration. When you eat an animal you are ingesting the vibration of that animal and if it had an unhappy life, that vibration is now in your body. And it gets stored in your body. Lots of these animals are kept in very cruel conditions that are bred solely for meat. If I was eating meat now, I would be supporting a local farmer whose animals get to see the sun and run around and experience joy, before they are eventually killed for meat.

One thing that is always mentioned to me that we can do to raise the vibration of our food and then in turn ourselves, is bless our food before we eat it. This really is an important thing. The gratitude you feel as you bless your food raises the vibration of the food. It also has a positive effect on you as a person as you are stopping to give thanks for what you have.

Feel true thanks for the sustenance that you are about to ingest.
It keeps you alive.
It allows your physical body to support you through life and keeps you functioning.
Focus on the taste and the texture and the pleasure you feel eating it.
Feel true gratitude.
You are blessed to have food to eat.

Lifestyle changes

Check your products that you use daily on your body and those that you ingest inside your body.

> Shampoo
> Conditioner
> Deodorants
> Toothpaste
> Shower Gel
> Hair gel
> Hairspray
> Makeup

Ensure that these products that you put on your skin day in and day out and ingest in your body are Aluminum free. You do not want Aluminum on your skin or in your body. It is this that makes its way to your Pineal Gland and in combination with the Fluoride in the water and toothpaste calcifies it. In other words it shuts it down. It stops your Pineal gland from working. Your Pineal gland is your gateway within yourself to the higher realms. You want this to be able to work.

Check all of your normal products that you use. How many of these products contain Aluminum or Fluoride? Get into the habit of starting to check products for their list of ingredients before you buy them. Inside of picking something for the brand or the packaging, pick something because it is going to help you raise your vibration.

Relaxation

In our busy lives today we have forgotten how to relax. We are always taught 'time is money' 'the early bird catches the worm' 'no pain no gain' and a variety of other phrases parroted at us by well-meaning people encouraging us to constantly be on the run.

 We have forgotten how to relax. We have forgotten how to close our eyes, be quiet and just be. It is when you are in this state of relaxation that your profoundest ideas will come to you. They will just drop in your head. As you have given them the space they need to arrive.

Our bodies are so used to being stressed and dashing from one place to another that we have forgotten how to listen to them.

We push our bodies until we sprain ankles, damage ligaments, rip muscles and suffer exhaustion.

We don't have time to face our emotions and because of this we manifest disease within our bodies.

We are encouraged to push ourselves to the limit in order to reach the heady heights of success, losing touch with the knowledge that success is already inside of you. And you have the power to manifest it. You hold everything you need for success inside of you and you can reach it through the power of visualisation.

One of the things that comes through very strongly in my sessions is that we need to slow down and relax! It is hard in the world that we live in as we always have to be somewhere for a certain time. Whether it is work or getting the kids to school or 'appointments.' We rush ourselves into exhaustion. We have to take time out to relax. Whether this is through undertaking a new hobby which allows you the opportunity to relax such as Yoga, Reiki, Crystal healing to name but a few, or whether it is from practicing Meditation.

Introduce some way into your life where you 'make time' to relax. This is a very, very important part of raising your vibration and for your whole wellbeing in general. People often overlook this for themselves. Myself included. I am a very busy person. I have two beautiful young children who need my full attention and I am also a Wife, a Quantum Healing Practitioner, an Author and I have a YouTube channel. I know how important it is to make time to be quiet and meditate and connect with your spirit guides and higher self. But some days I am so exhausted from being all of the above things that I just fall to sleep in a pile of dribble at the end of the day.

BUT, since I have started to carve out this time for myself (most) days. I have started to see my life change before my eyes. I am calmer. More peaceful. More full of joy. More grounded. More connected. Whatever it is that you do to relax. Make sure you integrate it into your daily life. Make time for you.

Ideas for relaxation

- Meditate for 15 minutes every day. When you practice meditation regularly, you will start to want to meditate longer than this but 15 minutes is a good place to start.
- Sit in the garden or in nature with your back against a tree for 15 minutes. The tree will naturally raise your frequency to be in tune with that of the Earth. The Earth has its own frequency. If you look up the latest Schumann Resonance frequency online. This is normally a good indication of whether there is an energy wave coming in or a solar storm as the increase in energy is reflected in the Schumann Resonance. I always know when the Schumann Resonance is spiking as I feel very tired. This gives us an indication that our planet and ourselves are linked. We are! We are all one.

- Relax with your planet and re-tune your individual frequency to hers
- Have a bath. Immersing yourself in water transmutes any negative frequencies that you may have been holding in your auric fields. Much like when you use crystals and you cleanse them in water. I transmute so much negative energy on a daily basis being an empath and doing the work that I do. I would go as far as to say I 'require' a bath daily in order to function. If I do not get one I can get a little cranky! After 30 minutes in the bath relaxing, I feel like a new woman. Refreshed, revitalized. Combine this with Epsom salts and you are on to a winner! Add in some relaxing music and crystals round the bath? Now that to me is heaven!
- Whatever it is that you enjoy that relaxes you. This is different things for different people. First you need to identify what it is. Then you need to make time for it daily. If you are adding daily relaxation into your life, you will be vibrating high in no time!

Meditation

This leads nicely into Meditation. What is Meditation? You can do guided Meditation where you sit in a comfortable place. Ideally use the same space daily as you will anchor incredible energies to this space as a result. And you sit and close your eyes. You can be cross legged or just sat up straight with your back against a wall, whatever you like. And then you can listen to a guided Meditation on YouTube and they will take you through what you need to do.

You can also simply just sit and be. And listen to what the Universe wants to tell you. This is an excellent way to link with your spirit guides and access your higher self and even Source itself. In order to do this you simply sit and concentrate on your breathing. Concentrate on how it feels to draw a breath in and then a breath out. Slow down your breathing and take your breath right the way down into your diaphragm. Feel how delicious it feels to draw in the oxygen into your lungs and then release it. If you mind starts to chatter, let it, it will quieten eventually. You can count your breaths from 1 up to 20 if you wish or you can just sit and breathe and see what comes to you. Be aware of what you can see in your 'mind's eye.' What is it trying to show you? Be aware of what guidance you receive.

You can also guide yourself through a Meditation in your mind. This is what I like to do. I like to go to my peaceful place in my house where I meditate. Then I sit cross legged and get comfortable. And I start to breathe deeply and take oxygen deep into my lungs. I then (in my mind) draw white light down from Source as my protection when I meditate. I imagine it all around me in a protective cloak. I also imagine it passing down my body through my crown chakra and as it passes through my body right the way down to my feet.

I imagine it cleaning all of the negativity out of my body and cleansing all of my chakras so they are working optimally. Once the white light has passed through my body, I then imagine the white light passing into the Earth and right the way down to Earth's core. I then picture the white light cleaning and strengthening the Earth's Core and I shoot a wave of love from my heart into that white light and down to the Earth. I tell the Earth that I love her, and how grateful I am that she allowed us to live on her surface to learn our lessons. I ask her if she has any message for me and how I can help her. When I have finished conversing with Gaia. I bring my attention back to my heart space. I feel gratitude for everything. Absolutely everything. My life. The opportunity to experience everything I do in physical form daily. I feel gratitude for my family. My loved ones, my friends. I feel gratitude for all of the lessons I have had in my life, even the hard ones as they have made me grow. They have made me the person that I am today. I send love out to everyone on Gaia. And finally I picture the Earth cleansed by the power of the energies coming in and sparkling with White light. I picture her fully of Light and Love and Happiness. I picture a world full of happiness where there are no children dying or starving hungry. I picture peace. I picture harmony. I picture Love. I picture the New Earth. I picture what I want to see and experience. I do not picture what I don't want to happen as whatever you visualise you manifest. So I picture what I do want to see happen. If more of us did this on a daily basis. Visualising the Earth as we want to see it, we would draw it to us quicker. Everything in thought eventually manifests in the physical. If you asked me what is one thing that you can do to help Earth right now, I would tell you meditate and picture heaven on Earth. Heaven on Earth will come.

But if we all did this. It would arrive quicker. The power of the collective consciousness and manifestation on Earth has yet to be realised by the masses. It is us that holds the power to shape our reality.

Crystals

When I meditate I like to hold a crystal. Crystals hold a very high vibration and also are one dimensional beings. You can program them to help you achieve what you want to achieve and they are excellent for merging their vibrational field with yours and allowing you to reach higher levels of consciousness. I am not ashamed to say that I own hundreds of crystals. They are friends to me and I speak to them as if they are such. I cleanse them after every use and I always ask their permission to use them for any task and if they would like to do it. There are so many crystals I would not know where to start in terms of telling you about them all, but I will tell you about my favourites and what I use crystals for.

Like I said earlier, I use crystals when I meditate. Prior to meditation I hold the crystal and I tell the crystal what I would like to achieve throughout the meditation and ask if it would be willing to help me. Then when I meditate I simply hold the crystal and the high vibrational energy that the crystal holds will help me to raise my vibration and access the higher realms and therefore the wisdom that I need.

I use crystals for healing. I use crystals for cleansing the chakras. I also use crystals in my Quantum Healing Sessions and my clients have the option to choose what crystals they want to work with. I personally choose to use a huge, palm, Selenite Stone to hold when I am hypnotising people. You have to be careful not to cleanse Selenite in water though as it melts away into the water. Cleanse Selenite with incense, or placing in the sunshine. My clients also have the choice of holding Selenite, Amethyst, Lapis Lazuli or Rose Quartz for the session.

I have a huge Black Tourmaline which is a powerful protection stone for negativity and dark entities and also for grounding clients back into their bodies.

I also use Shungite wands to ground my clients back into their bodies after a session. Shungite is an excellent stone for grounding.

My house is gridded with crystals. What do I mean by this? I have set up a crystal grid in my house to both raise the energies of the space and for protection. I have Black Tourmaline in the four furthest corners of my home and a clear quartz crystal pointing into the Tourmaline. The quartz channels the energy and the Tourmaline traps the negative energy.

I have crystals on every window sill. Rose Quartz in my relationship corner. Citrine in my wealth corner. A tiger's eye in the middle of my house. Amethyst in my bedroom. Celestine next to my bed. I have Giant Orgonites all over my house. Orgonites are crystals and copper/metal incased in resin and are excellent for raising the energy in your home and dispelling negative energy or EMF's changing them to positive energy. My home is covered in them! Not only are they beautiful to look at (if you get the nice homemade ones) but they actually raise the vibration of your home!

Crystals and High Vibration come hand in hand. In all of my Quantum Healing Sessions when clients end up on spaceships and from different planets, more often than not they will tell me that their space crafts are powered by crystals.

In the times of Atlantis, the people there understood how powerful crystals were and they were using them in their society. In one of my Quantum Healing Sessions I had a client who went to a life in Atlantis and she saw herself swimming with the Mermaids underwater. She was able to do this as she had on a Turquoise Necklace that enabled her to breathe underwater!

The ancient Egyptians were obsessed with crystals and in particular Lapis Lazuli. This is because they were aware of the power of crystals in enabling one to access higher levels of consciousness. The Egyptians would always be seen wearing pieces of Lapis and Turquoise.

All the evidence is there throughout the history books and ancient artifacts to prove that the ancients before us understood the power of crystals.

When you place crystals in your home in a nice clean space, you will feel the vibration of your home rise.

You will also notice that a lot of the lower vibrational creatures are no longer able to enter your space. Since I have had my house gridded wasps are unable to enter my home. They are repelled by the energies. If one manages to get in through the roof and falls into the house. It is disabled within seconds of entering the space. It is like they are drugged and can no longer fly. The higher vibration of the space disables their bodies. Last summer we had a couple of wasps get into our bathroom through the roof space and I found them in the bath later that night with their back ends exploded. It seems that my house has too many crystals for wasps to function!

When you are choosing crystals it is wise to pick them up and get a feel for if they are for you. You will pick five pieces of Amethyst up and one of those pieces will 'feel' like it is meant for you.

Also crystals are just like us. They get tired and need a rest. You must cleanse them after every use. And if your house is gridded with crystals, have a 'spare' grid that can be cleansing whilst the other is 'working.' That way you can refresh your main grid frequently and keep those energies high!

Smell

When I cleanse my crystals, I cleanse them with incense. The smell of incense always raises my vibration as it brings me joy. Allow smell to be a tool in your workbag to raise your vibration on a daily basis. What are your favourite smells? Do you like the smell of fresh flowers? Do you like the smell of essential oils? Do you like fragranced candles? Do you like the smell of freshly baked bread? Whatever you enjoy smelling, allow this consciously to play more of a role in your everyday life.

I have to burn incense daily in my home. It raises the vibration in my home instantly as it cleanses the crystals who then in turn vibrate higher and they affect everyone who lives in the house. The smell of the incense burning brings joy to my senses. It makes me feel happy. And if you are happy, you guessed it, your vibration rises!

Music

Music has the power to raise our vibration instantly. Good quality music. Classical music is fantastic for this. Anything that you listen to that causes you to feel joy, pure joy is raising your vibration.

There are also healing modalities that use sound for healing. Crystal Singing Bowls for example.

Gong Baths are also an excellent way of healing through sound.

The sounds of Nature whilst you are sat outside listening to the birds singing and the decadent sound of a river running over glossy, smooth pebbles.

Singing to yourself in the shower raises your vibration! No really it does! That's why you do it! As you sing in the shower and concentrate on the beautiful feeling of the warm water hitting your skin. Imagine the water is pure white light from Source and that as you are showering and singing you are washing all of your negativity away!

Service to Others (Kindness)

One of the quickest ways you can raise your frequency is to be in the frequency of Love.

Practicing kindness in your daily life. Showing kindness to not just your fellow human beings, but to every single being that you encounter. Looking for ways to help others. Looking for ways to be of Service to others. Thinking outside of yourself and your own insular needs and looking at the bigger picture. If we are all one then helping someone else is helping yourself. Having a wider perspective and a drive and desire to help others outside of yourself. Be approachable. Smile at people. Radiate love to such a point that people look at you thinking 'what is it that she/he's so happy about.' Help out in your community. Support local businesses. Recommend people that you've come across that have great skills to your friends. Share knowledge. Have compassion. Have empathy. If you see some rubbish on our planet – pick it up. I am obsessed with doing this when I am out and about. My young daughters have grown up thinking that is normal. That we must look after our planet and that if some 'naughty people' have dropped some rubbish whilst we are out walking, we pick it up and place it in the recycling bin. Have an awareness of caring for others. Have an awareness of caring for your planet. She has given herself to this task so that we may have a planet to learn our lessons on. Let's treat her with the respect that she so greatly deserves. Do not look to others to do this. Let this change start with **you**.

Nature

We need to reconnect with our planet. Our beautiful, breathtakingly beautiful planet. We need to reconnect with all of the gorgeous creatures on our planet.

When we are out in nature in our natural environment, we are in tune with our planets frequency and as a result we become more at ease.

Every client that comes to see me says under hypnosis that we are not spending enough time outside. We are losing ourselves. We are losing touch with our planet. We are spending each day getting up, going to work, working, coming home, eating, watching TV and then going to bed. Watching TV does not raise our frequency. Particularly with the content of most of it being very bleak these days and focusing on murders and darkness.

I am told we should be outside as much as we can be on any given day. Ideally shoes and socks off and allowing your feet to absorb the grounding energies of our planet. So we are in step with our planet. So we are the same frequency as our planet. If you are feeling negative and down, if you take off your shoes and socks and have a walk on the beach or on the grass and breathe deeply into your lungs, within minutes you will be feeling much better.

Trees are an excellent way to raise your vibration to that of the planet. Sit with your back to a tree and allow it to alter your auric field and vibrational frequency to be in tune with the Earth's.

The oceans of the planet help lift your frequency. There is consciousness in the water that transmutes negativity. I have come across this in my Quantum Healing Sessions. The water actually transmutes negativity. So if you want to raise your vibration, go and have a swim!

Heal Your Shadow

We all of us have experienced trauma and sorrow both in this life and in every incarnation we have ever had.

It seems inconceivable to us whilst we are here that we would sign up for some of the traumas that we have experienced, yet everything that happens in this realm is done with the agreement of our higher selves in order for the growth of our soul.

That being said, when we experience these traumas and tragedies in our physical incarnations, they are real, they are painful and they are scary. And some of these traumas wound us so deeply that we struggle to get over them.

People have unhealed trauma that they have experienced from this incarnation piling on top of prior unhealed trauma that was experienced in previous incarnations. And in view of that, there are people that have some incredibly deep layers of pain to heal.

It is essential that each one of these layers of pain are acknowledged, felt, healed and released in order for the trapped energy to be released from your body. Each time you face your darkest fears or deepest hurts and find the lesson and heal yourself, you are raising your vibration. That is why Quantum Healing or Past Life Regression is such a fantastic healing modality as it shows you where your trapped hurt is in your previous incarnations so you can acknowledge it and heal from it. For some people they carry round fears and phobias and anxieties all their lives and they do not know where they have come from. I regress them through hypnosis and we will always find the root cause.

Therefore this can then be acknowledged and healed and the client is set free from a cage they never even knew they were in. They can finally live the rest of their lives. I cannot recommend enough the power of Quantum Healing in terms of raising your vibration. It raises the vibration of your entire journey through time and existence! You are given a new lease of life. You are given new joy that resonates throughout your entire being.

Gratitude

Gratitude has changed my life. Throughout my 20's I was a very angry young woman due to the hand that life had dealt me. I felt everyone was out to get me and I couldn't understand why the things that happened to me did. Now I look back with the spiritual eyes that I have and I realise that every single thing that I experienced was for my highest good in terms of soul growth and it has got me where I am today and I wouldn't change my journey for the world no matter how hard it has been at times.

I was recommended a book by friends of mine at the time. I'm sure most of you will have read it. The Secret by Rhonda Byrne. And this fantastic book – changed my life. I have since the day I read that book practiced Gratitude in my daily life as a matter of course. To the point that now I have my brain so well trained that I am grateful for everything.

I am grateful for the first lung full of air in a morning and the delicious stretch. The feel of carpet under my feet as I pad down to collect my babies. The feel of their little arms around my neck as I lift them out of their cots. Their fluffy little morning heads and warm snuggly kisses. I am grateful for my morning coffee and the flavor of it which is so rich it makes my taste buds sing. I am grateful for the first swallow of crisp fresh water with a slice of lemon. I am grateful to be waking up in a house as opposed to cold and on the streets. I am grateful I have food to eat for breakfast. I am grateful just to be alive and on this planet. Planet Earth at the time of Ascension. The greatest show in the Cosmos and we have front row seats! What a time to be alive!

The list goes on and on and on.

I would strongly suggest keeping a Gratitude Journal. Every time you feel Gratitude in your life, write it down. Give thanks for what you are grateful for. Because if you do – the Universe always gives you more!

Joy

Can you remember the last time that you felt gleeful? Like really gleeful like when you were a child?

What were the things that used to make you feel happy when you were a child?

Children feel joy over the slightest things. All things for them hold joy. Twisting, running, jumping, playing with water, laughing, crayoning.

Whatever it is that's makes you feel the most joyful that you have ever felt – this is what you need to spend more time doing.

When you are in Joy you are in your highest vibration.

To raise your vibration do something that makes you truly happy as often as possible.

Being creative is also a really good way to enjoy yourself and raise your vibration. Do you like painting or writing or colouring. Do you like gardening or decorating. What sports do you enjoy? Whatever brings you joy – do as much of it as possible!

Final Thoughts

There are so many ways you can raise your vibration and if you tackle all of the areas mentioned in this book you will be well on your way to vibrating high.

A good way to indicate how you are vibrating is to examine how you are feeling. Your emotions will always tell you. Are you feeling Love? Are you feeling Joy? Are you feeling true Happiness? If so then you are vibrating high. Anything that is making you feel sad or angry is an indication that this is not for your highest good.

Your emotions are indicators for you to tell if you are on the right track. Listen to your emotions and listen to your body. Listen to your intuition. It will lead you in the right direction.

I would suggest keeping a dream journal and writing down what you are experiencing in your dreams. Our dreams often have incredible insights for us with regards to the changes we should be making in our daily lives. Any thoughts that you have, write them down and analyse them. Keep a gratitude journal. Eat good quality fresh fruit and vegetables. Drink water that is fluoride free. Get out in nature. Feel gratitude. Practise kindness for all creatures who share our planet. Switch off your TV's and put your phones to one side and go and meditate and connect with your spirit guides and higher self.

Now is the time to make the changes.
Do a little bit every day and before you know it you will be vibrating so high and smiling so wide that everyone will want to know what your secret is!

As we continue ever onwards on our Earth, it is abundantly clear that things cannot carry on the way that they have been.

We have to start looking after our planet and all of the creatures on it.

We cannot continue to start wars and hurt and torture people.

The people that understand this can see that there is a better way.

We can see a planet where all children are protected and everyone lives in peace.

We can see a planet where all creatures are respected and no one has to live in fear for their lives.

We can see a planet where we are all connected in love and we work together for the harmony and greatest good of all of the beings on the planet.

That is the planet we want to live on.

And that is the 5D Earth that we are manifesting right now.

With every single act of kindness you do for another creature or human on this Earth you are bringing that 5D Planet closer.

Be the change that you want to see on Earth.

We ARE the Light.

Laura Whitworth

Printed in Great Britain
by Amazon

44291796R00030